Thinking Critically: Obesity

Other titles in the *Thinking Critically* series include:

Thinking Critically

Thinking Critically: Obesity

Andrea C. Nakaya

ReferencePoint
Press®

San Diego, CA

© 2018 ReferencePoint Press, Inc.
Printed in the United States

For more information, contact:
ReferencePoint Press, Inc.
PO Box 27779
San Diego, CA 92198
www.ReferencePointPress.com

Picture Credits:
Charts and graphs by Maury Aaseng

LIBRARY OF CONGRESS CATALOGING-IN-PUBLICATION DATA

Name: Nakaya, Andrea C., 1976-
Title: Thinking critically: obesity / by Andrea C. Nakaya.
Description: San Diego, CA : ReferencePoint Press, Inc., 2018. | Series: Thinking critically series |
    Audience: Grade 9 to 12. | Includes bibliographical references and index.
Identifiers: LCCN 2016052555 (print) | LCCN 2016053617 (ebook) | ISBN 9781682822678
    (hardback) | ISBN 9781682822685 (eBook)
Subjects: LCSH: Obesity--United States--Juvenile literature.
Classification: LCC RC628 .N35 2018 (print) | LCC RC628 (ebook) | DDC 362.1963/98--dc23
LC record available at https://lccn.loc.gov/2016052555

Contents

Foreword

"Literacy is the most basic currency of the knowledge economy we're living in today." Barack Obama (at the time a senator from Illinois) spoke these words during a 2005 speech before the American Library Association. One question raised by this statement is: What does it mean to be a literate person in the twenty-first century?

E.D. Hirsch Jr., author of *Cultural Literacy: What Every American Needs to Know*, answers the question this way: "To be culturally literate is to possess the basic information needed to thrive in the modern world. The breadth of the information is great, extending over the major domains of human activity from sports to science."

But literacy in the twenty-first century goes beyond the accumulation of knowledge gained through study and experience and expanded over time. Now more than ever literacy requires the ability to sift through and evaluate vast amounts of information and, as the authors of the Common Core State Standards state, to "demonstrate the cogent reasoning and use of evidence that is essential to both private deliberation and responsible citizenship in a democratic republic."

The *Thinking Critically* series challenges students to become discerning readers, to think independently, and to engage and develop their skills as critical thinkers. Through a narrative-driven, pro/con format, the series introduces students to the complex issues that dominate public discourse—topics such as gun control and violence, social networking, and medical marijuana. All chapters revolve around a single, pointed question such as Can Stronger Gun Control Measures Prevent Mass Shootings?, or Does Social Networking Benefit Society?, or Should Medical Marijuana Be Legalized? This inquiry-based approach introduces student researchers to core issues and concerns on a given topic. Each chapter includes one part that argues the affirmative and one part that argues the negative—all written by a single author. With the single-author format the predominant arguments for and against an issue can be synthesized into clear, accessible discussions supported by details and evidence including relevant facts, direct quotes, current examples, and statistical illustrations. All volumes include focus questions to guide students as they read each pro/con discussion, a list of key facts, and an annotated list of related organizations and websites for conducting further research.

The authors of the Common Core State Standards have set out the particular qualities that a literate person in the twenty-first century must have. These include the ability to think independently, establish a base of knowledge across a wide range of subjects, engage in open-minded but discerning reading and listening, know how to use and evaluate evidence, and appreciate and understand diverse perspectives. The new *Thinking Critically* series supports these goals by providing a solid introduction to the study of pro/con issues.

Obesity

Americans are becoming larger. In 2015 data visualizer Max Galka used government information on body measurements and clothes sizing in the United States to understand how body size has changed over time. He looked at sizing records dating back to 1958 and found that many manufacturers have labeled clothing with progressively smaller size numbers. For instance, a current size 8 dress is almost the equivalent of a size 16 dress back then. A size 8 dress from 1958 would be smaller than a size 00 today.

When Galka analyzed Centers for Disease Control and Prevention (CDC) body measurement data, he found that the average American woman now weighs about as much as the average man did in the 1960s. Overall, his research reveals that Americans are significantly bigger than they were fifty years ago. In fact, an increasing number of men, women, and children are so big that they are defined as obese. Obesity is not confined to the United States, however; it has become increasingly prevalent all over the world. This has provoked widespread concern, and there is extensive debate over just how serious obesity is, what causes it, and whether society can successfully reduce obesity levels.

Defining Obesity

The human body is like a machine that requires energy to run. People consume calories through food and beverages, and their bodies convert those calories into energy through a process called metabolism. If the body does not use up all the calories that are consumed, it stores the excess as fat. All bodies process and store calories differently, and the process is influenced by many factors, including genetics, levels of physical activity, and even exposure to environmental chemicals. Overall, though, when people consistently consume more calories than they use, over time the amount of fat in their bodies increases, and they can become overweight and then obese.

Whether a person has enough body fat to qualify as obese is usually determined by calculating his or her body mass index (BMI). BMI is a measurement of weight in relation to height. It is the most common way medical professionals estimate a person's body fat. It is calculated by dividing weight in kilograms by height in meters squared. For pounds and inches, BMI can be calculated by dividing a person's weight in pounds by his or her height in inches squared, then multiplying by a conversion factor of 703. For adults, a BMI below 18.5 is considered underweight, from 18.5 to 24.9 is normal, from 25.0 to 29.9 is overweight, and 30.0 and above is obese. BMI is interpreted differently for young people because their weight and height change as they grow. In the United States BMI for a young person is expressed as a percentile, which is an interpretation of BMI relative to other children of the same age and gender. A child is classified as overweight if his or her BMI is between the 85th and 94th percentile and as obese if it is at or above the 95th percentile.

Some people are critical of using BMI to measure obesity. This is because it does not account for the distribution of body fat, and distribution is an important part of determining how fat affects a person's health. Fat around the abdominal area is correlated with more health risks than fat in other areas. In addition, a BMI measurement does not differentiate between a person who has a lot of body fat and a person who has a lot of muscle, like an athlete. However, despite these flaws, health care professionals have found BMI to be a useful guide, and it is the most common method for evaluating whether a person is overweight or obese.

A Common Condition

Obesity rates have increased dramatically in recent years and are very high for both adults and young people in the United States and all over the world. The CDC reports that in the United States, about 37 percent

Adult Obesity in the United States

Obesity remains a serious health concern in much of the United States. The states with the highest rates of adult obesity, according to the latest statistics available, are Louisiana, Mississippi, Alabama, and West Virginia. Louisiana's rate of 36.2 percent is the highest in the nation. The state with the lowest adult obesity rate is Colorado, at 20.2 percent. Four states—Montana, Minnesota, Ohio, and New York—have experienced decreases in adult obesity rates, and two others—Kansas and Kentucky—have seen increases, but the remaining states have changed little between 2014 and 2015.

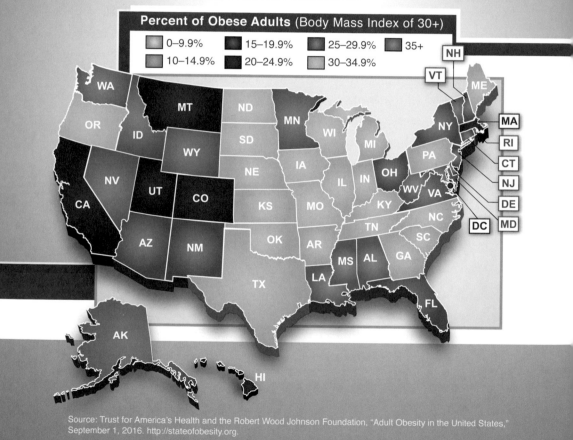

Percent of Obese Adults (Body Mass Index of 30+)

- 0–9.9%
- 10–14.9%
- 15–19.9%
- 20–24.9%
- 25–29.9%
- 30–34.9%
- 35+

Source: Trust for America's Health and the Robert Wood Johnson Foundation, "Adult Obesity in the United States," September 1, 2016. http://stateofobesity.org.

of adults and 17 percent of young people ages two to nineteen are obese. In addition, a large number are overweight, meaning that the majority of the US population is classified as either overweight or obese.

According to the World Health Organization's (WHO) most recent report, in 2014, 39 percent of the world's adults were overweight, and 13 percent—or more than 600 million—were obese. The agency also finds that 41 million children under age five are overweight or obese. WHO says that worldwide, obesity has more than doubled since 1980. WHO reports that in the past, obesity was mainly a problem for high-income countries, but it is now a serious issue in many low- and middle-income countries too. For example, between 1990 and 2014, the number of overweight or obese children in Africa nearly doubled. As a result, WHO and other organizations, like the Center for Science in the Public Interest (CSPI), conclude that obesity is now a worldwide issue. "Obesity has become a global problem," stated the authors of a 2016 CSPI report. "With the exception of some countries in sub-Saharan Africa, practically every country in the world faces daunting obesity rates."[1]

While most nations are trying to reduce these rates, obesity has become so widespread that many are also taking action to adapt to a future where obesity is common. Robert Paarlberg, a researcher on food and agricultural policy, gives examples of how the United States is adapting to accommodate increasingly large body sizes. He says:

> Office chairs once rated for no more than 300 pounds are now being replaced with new products ($1,300 each) that can handle up to 600 pounds. Some hospitals have spent up to $5 million to accommodate the obese with supersized beds, open MRI machines, and toilets bolted to the floor instead of the wall. Funeral homes now offer much larger caskets. Movie theater seats are six inches wider than they were in the 1980s, revolving doors two feet wider, and more automobiles today have rear-view cameras, good for safety but also convenient for drivers who cannot turn around.[2]

According to the Gallup organization, polls indicate there are also increasingly fewer people who want to lose weight. The organization reports that in 2015, about half of Americans said they would like to lose weight, down from almost 60 percent in surveys conducted between 2001 and 2008.

Consequences of Obesity

There is disagreement over the extent to which obesity threatens society. Many insist that the increasing prevalence and acceptance of obesity have a number of negative consequences. Among the most concerning are the health problems associated with obesity. Being obese increases a person's risk of heart disease, stroke, diabetes, and some types of cancer. These are leading causes of death in the United States. Obesity is also associated with numerous other health conditions, including arthritis, high cholesterol, sleep apnea and other breathing problems, and mental health problems like depression and anxiety. In addition, people who are obese frequently report that they face stigma and discrimination and overall have a reduced quality of life. However, others contend that the health threats of obesity have been greatly exaggerated and that many obese people are actually quite healthy.

> "We *really* don't want to be fat. So why are we?"[4]
>
> —John Hoffman, Judith A. Salerno, and Alexandra Moss, authors of *The Weight of the Nation: To Win We Have to Lose*

In addition to numerous health consequences, obesity has substantial economic costs. Obesity researchers Ping Zhang, Sundar S. Shrestha, and Rui Li investigated the economic costs of obesity in the United States and a number of other countries and found that in the United States, obesity results in medical costs that are 37 percent to 42 percent higher than for people with a normal body weight. In other countries, costs were estimated to be 12 percent to 48 percent higher. The authors conclude, "A substantial amount of economic costs to health-care systems, employers, governments, individuals, and the nation could be avoided if we succeeded in lowering the prevalence of obesity."[3] CDC data also show that obesity has a substantial economic cost. According to the agency's most recent estimate, obesity's annual medical cost is $147 billion.

Continuing Debate

There is considerable debate over exactly why obesity rates are higher than ever before. In the past, obesity was generally blamed on individuals and their failure to maintain a healthy weight through good diet and exercise.

However, while poor diet and lack of exercise undoubtedly contribute to obesity, many critics have recently begun to argue that environment also affects a person's weight. Some people believe that in the United States and elsewhere, certain environmental forces are making it extremely difficult for individuals to make healthy diet and exercise choices. For example, many people do not get much exercise because they have long commutes and work in sedentary jobs. Large numbers of people also eat high-calorie fast-food meals because these are inexpensive and less time-consuming than cooking a meal from scratch. Together, these factors and forces are often referred to as an obesogenic environment.

Overall, the United States and other nations invest considerable resources in understanding and reducing obesity. Yet these efforts have been largely unsuccessful, and obesity levels continue to rise. As the authors of *The Weight of the Nation* point out, it is an issue of great concern to many people. They state, "We spend more than $40 billion every year on diet products and services, trying *not* to be fat—that's not a little concern, that's more than the GDP (gross domestic product) of half the world's nations. We *really* don't want to be fat. So why are we?"[4] The issue of obesity remains complex and extremely controversial. All around the world, widespread debate continues about what is causing it, how serious the issue is, and what society should do about it.

Chapter One

Does Obesity Pose a Serious Health Threat?

Obesity Poses a Serious Health Threat

- Obesity causes numerous health problems, many of which are serious.
- Many obese people have a lower quality of life than people of normal weight.
- People with obesity often face stigma and discrimination.
- Obesity is such a serious problem that it should be considered an epidemic.

The Debate at a Glance

Obesity Does Not Pose a Serious Health Threat

- Obesity levels have been overestimated.
- While obesity has increased, health and life expectancy have improved for most people.
- There is no evidence that obesity causes health problems.
- Many obese people are also very healthy.

Obesity Poses a Serious Health Threat

"The United States faces an *epidemic of obesity*, an alarming rise that far exceeds levels for a healthy life. . . . It is having a severe impact on the health and wellbeing of Americans."

—Anna Bellisari, author of *The Anthropology of Obesity*

Anna Bellisari, *The Anthropology of Obesity in the United States*. New York: Routledge, 2016, p. 1.

Consider these questions as you read:

1. What three main health threats do you think are posed by obesity? In your opinion, why are these cause for concern?
2. Which pieces of evidence in this essay most strongly support the argument that obesity poses a serious health threat? Why do you think they are strong?
3. If being obese becomes more common than being of normal weight, how do you think this might threaten the United States in the future?

Editor's note: The discussion that follows presents common arguments made in support of this perspective, reinforced by facts, quotes, and examples taken from various sources.

Mirna "Minnie" Ortiz has type 2 diabetes. Ortiz is overweight, which makes type 2 diabetes more likely; but she had never heard of the condition until she was twelve years old and suddenly fell into a diabetic coma while sitting on her couch. "I was in a diabetic coma for week," says Ortiz. "I was fed through IVs because I wasn't allowed to eat. When I finally woke up, I was really disoriented because I didn't remember anything that had happened to me."[5]

In the past type 2 diabetes was called adult-onset diabetes because it was never seen in children. However, as the percentage of overweight and obese children has increased, this illness is becoming increasingly common in young people, and doctors worry they will face a lifetime of serious health problems. Type 2 diabetes is just one of the many obesity-related health conditions that pose a serious threat to individuals and society.

Diabetes

Ortiz's case is no exception; type 2 diabetes is strongly correlated with being obese. In fact, according to the National Institute of Diabetes and Digestive and Kidney Diseases, 80 percent of people with diabetes are overweight or obese. Diabetes is a serious problem in the United States. According to the CDC, more than 29 million Americans have diabetes—about 9.3 percent of the population. The majority of these cases are type 2. Between 1980 and 2012, the rate of adult diabetes almost quadrupled in the United States, causing the CDC to warn, "If this trend continues, as many as 1 out of every 3 adults in the United States could have diabetes by 2050."[6]

Diabetes has serious health implications. It is the seventh leading cause of death in the United States and the leading cause of adult-onset blindness, kidney failure, and lower-limb amputations. The CDC reports that more than 20 percent of health care spending in the United States is for people with diabetes. The threat of diabetes is not confined to the United States, however. According to a 2013 study by banking company Credit Suisse, type 2 diabetes is a global health threat, affecting almost 370 million people worldwide. It is projected to increase to almost 500 million by 2020, with health care costs reaching $700 billion globally every year.

Cancer and Other Diseases and Conditions

Obesity is associated with numerous other health conditions too, many of which are serious. The CDC reports that an obese person has a higher chance of developing high blood pressure, high cholesterol, coronary heart disease, gallbladder disease, osteoarthritis, and even cancer. According to a 2015 report by the State of Obesity, a project of the Trust for America's Health and the Robert Wood Johnson Foundation, up to 40 percent of cancers can be attributed to obesity, as well as between 24 percent and 34 percent of kidney disease cases. Obesity is also associated with an increased risk of stroke and with sleep apnea and other breathing problems.

Carrying a lot of weight can also result in numerous discomforts, such as mobility issues and joint problems, which make life more difficult. Another source of discomfort is arthritis, and the Obesity Action Coalition reports that a person who is obese is about 60 percent more likely than a person of normal weight to develop arthritis. The website Reddit contains numerous postings from people who face these kinds of daily struggles as a result of being obese. "Oh lord my knees," writes one person. "My joints have never been as tired or as sore as this in my life."[7] "You sweat, a lot, and you have no control over it," says another. "It's like wearing 2 extra sweaters wherever you go. . . . I could just WALK down a street corner and my entire shirt would be covered in sweat."[8] Another complains, "My feet kill me every day."[9]

> "If this trend continues, as many as 1 out of every 3 adults in the United States could have diabetes by 2050."[6]
>
> —Centers for Disease Control and Prevention

The Effects of Weight Stigma

In addition to physical problems like diabetes, obesity can also threaten a person's happiness and well-being and even cause mental health problems such as depression and anxiety. Numerous studies show that both children and adults who are obese are often treated unkindly or discriminated against. For example, overweight children are commonly teased, bullied, and ostracized by peers. According to the Obesity Action Coalition, negative attitudes toward obese children are seen as early as in preschool. According to the coalition, overweight children are often seen as bad people simply because they are overweight. It states, "Preschoolers report that their overweight peers are mean and less desirable playmates

Obesity Significantly Increases the Risk of Developing Diabetes

People who are obese are significantly more likely to develop diabetes than people who are of normal weight. This chart compares diabetes rates between people of normal weight and those who are obese. It shows that when a person is obese, he or she is much more likely to have diabetes. Overall, 21.7 percent of obese US adults have diabetes, while only 4.6 percent of those of normal weight do. From a statistical perspective, percentages are similar across different ethnic groups. Using these percentages, researchers also calculated the increased probability of being diagnosed with diabetes when one is obese. The chart shows that the average US adult is 4.7 times more likely to be diabetic if he or she is obese.

	Normal weight	Obese	Increased probabilty of diabetes diagnosis when obese
US adults	4.6%	21.7%	4.7x
Whites	4.4%	21.9%	5.0x
Blacks	5.9%	23.4%	4.0x
Hispanics	5.0%	18.7%	3.7x
Asians	3.1%	15.3%	4.9x

Source: Gallup, "US Obesity Rate Climbs to Record High in 2015," February 12, 2016. www.gallup.com.

compared to non-overweight children, and they believe that overweight children are mean, stupid, ugly, unhappy, lazy and have few friends."[10] The coalition reports that such attitudes only become more unkind as the children get older.

Obese adults similarly report being treated unkindly or unfairly simply because they are obese. For example, there is evidence that employers are less likely to hire obese individuals and that obese employees are often paid less. Studies have also shown that obese people have more trouble dating or finding a marriage partner. Gallup reports that obesity seems to be harmful to a person's well-being. In 2014 the organization surveyed almost eighty-five thousand US adults and found that those who were obese were less likely to be thriving socially. Such stigmatizing behavior is a major problem. "Taken together, the consequences of being denied jobs, rejected by peers and treated inappropriately by healthcare professionals because of one's weight can have a serious and negative impact on quality of life,"[11] notes the Obesity Action Coalition.

An Epidemic

Obesity affects so many people and rates are increasing so rapidly that many medical professionals have begun to refer to it as an epidemic. The National Institute of Diabetes and Digestive and Kidney Diseases says the prevalence of obese adults in the United States has more than doubled since 1960. In regard to this trend, medical doctor Robert H. Lustig warns, "For the . . . adults who are normal weight, pay attention. . . . A few years ago, you were the majority of Americans. Now you're the minority. And you're losing your percentage year by year."[12]

A similar trend has been observed among children. The CDC reports that in the past thirty years, obesity has more than doubled in children and quadrupled in adolescents. Obesity rates among minority children are even higher. For example, according to a report by the State of Obesity, about 3.3 percent of white boys are obese, but 10.1 percent of African American boys are.

Obesity rates among young people are rising so quickly that there will be significant impacts on society. Warns the State of Obesity: "If we fail to change the course of the nation's obesity epidemic, the current generation of young people may be the first in American history to live shorter, less healthy lives than their parents."[13] Nothing less than the nation's security may be at stake. Consider that the US military helps ensure the security and freedom of American citizens, and to perform that crucial role, its members must be physically fit and healthy. However, according to Mission: Readiness, an organization made up of retired military leaders, an increasing number of Americans are failing military weight standards. In fact, more than 27 percent of all Americans age seventeen to twenty-four are too heavy to join the military. In addition, Mission: Readiness finds that every year more than twelve hundred members of the military are discharged before their contracts are up because they weigh too much. The organization warns, "The United States military stands ready to protect the American people, but if our nation does not help ensure that future generations grow up to be healthy and fit, that will become increasingly difficult."[14]

Not Alone, but No Less in Trouble

While the United States has one of the highest obesity rates in the world, it is closely followed by many other countries. In fact, according to Helen Clark, administrator of the United Nations Development Programme, from 1908 to 2013 the worldwide prevalence of overweight and obese children rose by 47 percent and adults by 28 percent. "We now live in a world were 2.1 billion people—nearly one-third of the entire population—are overweight or obese,"[15] says Clark. Because it is so widespread and frequently causes significant health problems, obesity is one of the biggest challenges to public health that the world faces.

Obesity Does Not Pose a Serious Health Threat

"The data show there are tens of millions of people who are overweight and obese and are perfectly healthy."

—A. Janet Tomiyama, professor of psychology at the University of California, Los Angeles

Quoted in Stuart Wolpert, "Don't Use Body Mass Index to Determine Whether People Are Healthy, UCLA-Led Study Says," *UCLA Newsroom*, February 4, 2016. http://newsroom.ucla.edu.

Consider these questions as you read:

1. Do you agree that BMI is not a good way to evaluate a person's weight? Why or why not?
2. How strong is the argument that instead of being concerned that people weigh too much, society should celebrate the fact that people no longer suffer from starvation? Explain your answer.
3. Which pieces of evidence in this discussion provide the strongest support for the argument that obesity does not pose a serious health threat? Which provide the weakest support and why?

Editor's note: The discussion that follows presents common arguments made in support of this perspective, reinforced by facts, quotes, and examples taken from various sources.

Thirty-nine-year-old Mirna Valerio runs 35 miles (56 km) every week. She has completed six marathons, and six ultramarathons. However, she weighs 250 pounds (113 kg), and when people look at her, many automatically assume she is unhealthy. "People say, 'I don't understand why she's still fat. Obviously she has thyroid issues,'" says Valerio. "Or, I must have a terrible diet, and am I secretly sitting on my couch eating a gallon of ice cream?" Valerio insists that none of these are true—her body is just naturally larger than some other bodies. "That's the way my body is built, the way my family members are built," she says. "I'm never, ever gonna be whatever size people think I 'should' be."[16] As Valerio's story shows, it is commonly assumed that obesity comes with health problems. Some people point to the percentage of obese and overweight people in the United States and around the world and warn that society faces a serious health threat. In reality, many obese people do not have health problems, and the threat of obesity has been greatly exaggerated.

An Exaggerated Threat

Many experts believe that BMI—the measurement most commonly used to evaluate weight—is frequently inaccurate and that as a result, obesity rates in the United States and elsewhere have been overestimated. The problem with BMI is that it is a simple calculation of weight compared to height. This means it does not distinguish between weight that comes from muscle and weight that comes from fat. In this way, individuals who weigh a lot because they have a lot of muscle—such as athletes— can be classified as obese. The Center for Consumer Freedom insists that the BMI system makes no sense. "Are these classifications meaningful?" the center asks. "According to the government standard, Tom Cruise, Sylvester Stallone, and Mel Gibson are technically obese. So are sluggers Sammy Sosa and Barry Bonds, boxer Mike Tyson, quarterback Donovan McNabb, and wrestling superstar The Rock."[17] Therefore, a reliance on BMI can lead to an overestimation of obesity.

Not only are obesity rates likely overestimated, but data show that they are not continually rising, as some critics claim. For instance, according to the Robert Wood Johnson Foundation, childhood obesity has actually held steady or even decreased in some age groups in recent years. The organization reports that since 2003–2004, the obesity rate among children ages two to nine has stayed about the same. Among two- to five-year-olds, it decreased from almost 14 percent in 2003–2004 to about 9 percent in 2011–2014. Risa Lavizzo-Mourey, president and chief executive officer (CEO) of the Robert Wood Johnson Foundation, says, "This reinforces our confidence that America's children are moving toward a healthier weight, and that bodes well for the long-term health of our nation. I celebrate the message . . . that obesity rates for all children have remained level and are declining among the youngest kids. It's a sign that we are beginning to see a turn in the right direction."[18] CDC data also show a positive trend in obesity rates. The data indicate that while obesity among high school students has increased since 1991, since 2013 there has been no increase in the percentages of either obesity or overweight among high school students.

In fact, while critics worry that obesity rates are high and pose a serious health threat, the reality is that health has actually improved substantially for many people. For example, a 2014 report from the Fraser Institute, a research and educational organization, pointed out that while obesity might have increased, so has life expectancy. The report's authors write:

> **"Obesity rates for all children have remained level and are declining among the youngest kids. It's a sign that we are beginning to see a turn in the right direction."[18]**
>
> —Risa Lavizzo-Mourey, president and CEO of the Robert Wood Johnson Foundation

It is worth noting that, at the turn of the 20th century, average life expectancy was just 47 years; by the start of this decade, it had risen to 80 years, on average. The United Nations' demographers forecast that, by the dawn of the next century, the average American male will enjoy a life expectancy of 96.5 years, while the average female will have a life expectancy of precisely 100 years.[19]

Such a dramatic increase goes against arguments that rising obesity rates are seriously harming health.

The *Chattanooga Times Free Press* suggests that instead of being concerned that people weigh too much, society should celebrate the fact that people no longer suffer from starvation and malnutrition. "Throughout human history, the biggest challenge for man has been eating enough calories to work productively, fight off disease and not starve to death. But now . . . there is more than enough food to feed all the people on Earth."

Childhood Obesity Is Stabilizing

While some warn that childhood obesity is becoming worse every year, this graph shows that childhood obesity rates have actually held steady—at about 17 percent since 2004.

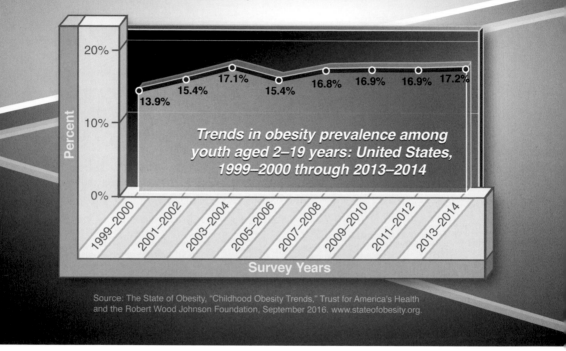

Trends in obesity prevalence among youth aged 2–19 years: United States, 1999–2000 through 2013–2014

Source: The State of Obesity, "Childhood Obesity Trends." Trust for America's Health and the Robert Wood Johnson Foundation, September 2016. www.stateofobesity.org.

The newspaper insists, "Rather than focusing on obesity, we should focus on the fact that people are being fed."[20] It points out that for the first time, more people in the world are obese than are hungry—and argues that is something society should celebrate, not worry about.

Obese and Healthy

Furthermore, there is no proof that obesity even causes health problems. For instance, in a study published in 2016 in the *International Journal of Obesity*, researchers examined the link between BMI and a number of measures of health, including blood pressure and cholesterol levels. They found that BMI was not a good predictor of a person's health. Almost half of the study participants who were overweight and 29 percent of those who were obese were metabolically healthy. However, a significant percentage of those who were considered to be at a normal weight according to their BMI were actually *unhealthy*. Overall, the researchers concluded that BMI is not a good way to evaluate whether a person is healthy. In a different study published in the *Journal of the American Medical Association* in 2013, researchers also examined the relationship between BMI and health; they too found a lack of evidence linking obesity and poor health. They analyzed numerous previous studies and found that overweight people and those in the lowest category of obesity did not have a higher incidence of mortality.

Instead, researchers stress that factors such as what individuals eat and their level of physical activity are far more important than weight for determining health. Dr. Andrew Weil, author of the natural health and wellness website Weil Lifestyle, insists, "The goal of optimum health is not to be thin, but to be as healthy as you can, regardless of weight. It's very clear to me that some people are genetically programmed to carry extra pounds, and as long as they maintain their cardiovascular health through exercise, they should indeed be considered healthy."[21] Glenn Gaesser, an exercise and wellness professor at Arizona State University, agrees. "What we're learning is that a body that exercises regularly is generally a healthy body, whether that body is fat or thin." As a result, he says, "The message should really be that if you are exercising regularly, you shouldn't necessarily be looking at the scale to determine how healthy or fit you are."[22]

Author Hanne Blank is an example of a person who is overweight but healthy. She says, "I'm out there almost every day, walking, biking, hiking, or weight lifting. I feel comfortable in my body. I'm energetic and healthy." However, she says that many people refuse to accept that this is possible and assume that if she is so active, she should not weigh so much. She says, "Even people close to me sometimes

> "What we're learning is that a body that exercises regularly is generally a healthy body, whether that body is fat or thin."[22]
>
> —Glenn Gaesser, an exercise and wellness professor at Arizona State University

shake their heads and ask why I'm still fat."[23] Blank insists that her body simply looks a certain way and that this is not a reflection of her health.

Fat acceptance activist Marilyn Wann complains that despite evidence to the contrary, society continues to assume that it is an anomaly to be both obese and healthy. She says, "In the medical literature, every time fat people prove to be healthier or to live longer than thin people, researchers call that result an 'obesity paradox.'" She insists that this is prejudicial and not supported by facts. "I'd call their refusal to view fat people positively a form of prejudice."[24] Like Wann, many critics believe that concerns about obesity have been exaggerated and insist it does not pose a serious threat to health.

Chapter Two

Is Obesity a Matter of Personal Responsibility?

Obesity Is a Matter of Personal Responsibility

- Weight is the result of the personal choices a person makes.
- Obesity is the result of eating too much and not exercising enough.
- Research shows that diet is not forced on people by their environment.
- As guardians and food gatekeepers, parents are responsible for their children's weight.

The Debate at a Glance

Obesity Is Not a Matter of Personal Responsibility

- Obesity is strongly influenced by genes.
- The modern environment causes obesity by making it easy to overeat and difficult to exercise.
- Environmental chemicals make obesity more likely.
- "Food deserts" contribute to obesity.

Obesity Is a Matter of Personal Responsibility

"Weight gain is simply eating more calories than you burn off. . . . Weight is a matter of individual lifestyle."

—J. Justin Wilson, senior research analyst at the Center for Consumer Freedom

J. Justin Wilson, "Obesity Is a Private Issue, Not a Public Epidemic," NJ.com, June 24, 2012. http://blog .nj.com.

Consider these questions as you read:

1. Do you agree with the argument that parents are responsible for whether their children are obese? Why or why not?
2. Do you think obesity rates in the United States would be lower if Americans spent more time exercising? Explain your answer.
3. Can a person choose *not* to become obese even if he or she is genetically predisposed to obesity? If so, how? If not, why not?

Editor's note: The discussion that follows presents common arguments made in support of this perspective, reinforced by facts, quotes, and examples taken from various sources.

When she was nine years old, Breanna Bond was obese. She weighed 186 pounds (84 kg) and struggled to move around comfortably. Her legs rubbed together so much when she walked that they chafed and bled. However, in less than a year, Breanna lost 65 pounds (29 kg) and soon after that reached her goal weight of 110 pounds (50 kg). Her mother, Heidi Bond, wrote a book about how she and her daughter worked together to overcome obesity. She insists that Breanna's transformation was the result of *deciding* that she would not be obese, then taking action to make it a reality. "Obesity is 100 percent treatable, fixable, and curable,"

Heidi says. "It takes dedication and hard work, but it is *not* a life sentence! My daughter is living proof that with a pair of tennis shoes and some motivation, you can choose a brand-new life."[25] While environmental and biological forces do influence weight, the Bonds' story shows that ultimately it is personal choice that determines how much a person weighs.

Diet and Exercise

One of the most common ways both young people and adults become obese is by making poor choices about what they eat. This is because diet is one of the most important factors in determining weight. If a person consumes more calories than his or her body needs, the excess is stored as fat; consistently consuming too many calories over a long period of time can thus lead to obesity.

To prove that obesity is the result of personal choices like eating too much, British television personality Katie Hopkins gained 42 pounds (19 kg) in three months, then lost it again. The 2015 documentary *Journey to Fat and Back* documents her process. Hopkins insists her weight gain was the result of choosing to consume far more food than her body needed. "One of the key messages [of this documentary] is that we tend to give people excuses all the time for being fat, but there are no excuses," she says. "If you eat too much and you don't move enough, then you get fat. But if you eat a bit less and you move a lot more, you can get rid of that weight again."[26]

> "Obesity is 100 percent treatable, fixable, and curable."[25]
>
> —Heidi Bond, whose daughter lost 65 pounds

As Hopkins argues, in addition to diet, lack of exercise is another key reason for obesity. Numerous studies have shown a correlation between obesity and a lack of exercise. The Harvard School of Public Health explains that exercise is an important part of regulating a person's weight. Overall, it says, "The more active people are, the more likely they are to keep their weight steady; the more sedentary, the more likely they are to gain weight over time."[27] Obesity statistics also show a correlation between obesity and a lack of exercise. For instance, according to a 2015 report by the State of Obesity, the four US states with the highest obesity rates also have the most adults who do not exercise. WHO finds that the majority of children worldwide do not exercise enough and argues this is a key reason for high obesity levels. It warns, "Low physical activity is rapidly becoming the social norm in most countries."[28] Overall, WHO reports that in 2010, 81 percent of eleven- to seventeen-year-olds did not engage in enough physical activity.

Parents Are Most Responsible

In the case of young people, much of the blame for obesity falls on parents, since many children lack the knowledge or maturity to make the healthy choices to maintain a normal weight. It is the parents' job to protect their children from becoming obese by teaching them to make good diet and exercise choices and helping them execute these decisions. That responsibility for childhood obesity lies with parents is the opinion of the majority of doctors. In fact, in 2015 SERMO, a global social network for physicians, conducted a poll of its members and received more than two thousand responses from doctors around the world. The majority agreed that parents are responsible for whether their children become obese. Only 1 percent said that parents are not to blame at all. "There's a reason why children live with parents until they become adults," says Debbie Gisonni, author and CEO of Professional BusinessWomen of California, an organization that works to empower women. "They aren't capable of taking care of themselves. Their brains aren't even fully developed until their mid-20s, so up until then, good judgment is compromised."[29]

> "If you eat too much and you don't move enough, then you get fat. But if you eat a bit less and you move a lot more, you can get rid of that weight again."[26]
>
> —Katie Hopkins, documentarian

Personal Choice Trumps Environment

Some critics argue that obesity is the result of living in an environment with too many fast-food restaurants and not enough healthy food options.

Most Adults Do Not Get Enough Exercise

People can avoid obesity if they eat well and get enough exercise—which most adults fail to do, according to the Centers for Disease Control and Prevention. Between 1997 and 2015, fewer than half of Americans age eighteen and over met the federal guidelines for aerobic exercise—because, it is argued, they chose not to.

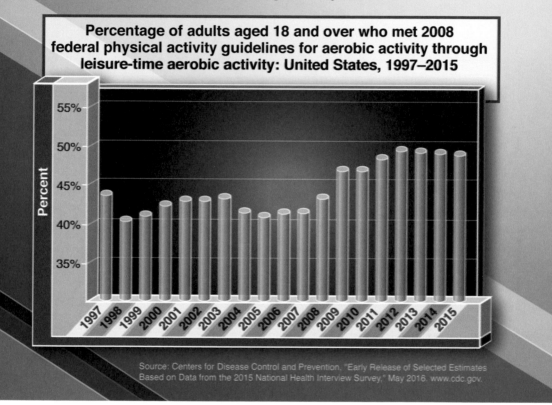

Percentage of adults aged 18 and over who met 2008 federal physical activity guidelines for aerobic activity through leisure-time aerobic activity: United States, 1997–2015

Source: Centers for Disease Control and Prevention, "Early Release of Selected Estimates Based on Data from the 2015 National Health Interview Survey," May 2016. www.cdc.gov.

However, a number of research studies have proved that people's diets are not forced on them by the environment and that the behavior that leads to obesity remains of the individual's choosing. For example, in a 2011 study published in the *Archives of Internal Medicine*, researchers used data from about five thousand people to analyze what they ate in relation to how close they lived to supermarkets and fast-food restaurants. The researchers found that access to supermarkets was not significantly related to the consumption of fruit and vegetables or to overall diet quality.

Steven Cummins, a professor of population health at the London School of Hygiene and Tropical Medicine, conducted another study investigating people's food choices. It focused on whether adding new stores in underserved Philadelphia communities influenced people's fruit and vegetable consumption and their obesity levels. He found it did not. "When given the opportunity, very few people try and switch to using newer or better provisions within their local community,"[30] Cummins said. Instead, he reports that while better supermarkets gave people the perception that things had gotten better in their neighborhood, their behavior did not change significantly.

To people like Christopher Snowdon, director of Lifestyle Economics at the Institute of Economic Affairs, this indicates that so-called environmental pressures either are not a factor in obesity or can be overcome through personal choice and determination. He points out that while obesity rates have risen, a large number of people are *not* obese, proving that people are capable of making choices to avoid obesity. He insists that every person has this ability—what differs is the extent to which they exercise it. "The evidence is all around us," Snowdon says. "Even in the United States, with its supposedly 'obesogenic' environment, two-thirds of adults and 83 percent of children are not obese."[31]

Many experts believe that personal choice and determination can even overcome a genetic predisposition to obesity. For example, the Harvard School of Public Health explains that while genes do influence whether a person becomes obese, research has shown that they only have a small influence. "Our genes are not our destiny," it insists. "Many people who carry these so-called 'obesity genes' do not become overweight, and healthy lifestyles can counteract these genetic effects."[32]

While a person's environment might influence the choices he or she makes, body weight is ultimately and fundamentally a matter of personal choice and responsibility. As nutritionist David Katz insists, "At the end of the day, what each of us does with our feet and our forks is up to us."[33]

Obesity Is Not a Matter of Personal Responsibility

"To blame obesity on the obese is the easy answer, but it is the *wrong* answer."

—Robert H. Lustig, a medical doctor

Robert H. Lustig, *Fat Chance: Beating the Odds Against Sugar, Processed Food, Obesity, and Disease*. New York: Hudson Street, 2012, p. xiii.

Consider these questions as you read:

1. In your experience, which environmental influences most significantly affect your diet and the amount you exercise?
2. For what purpose might humans be genetically programmed to over-eat? Do you think this is a plausible explanation for modern-day obesity? Why or why not?
3. Do you agree with the argument that obesity is caused by how close or far one lives to a grocery store? Why or why not?

Editor's note: The discussion that follows presents common arguments made in support of this perspective, reinforced by facts, quotes, and examples taken from various sources.

Until recently, the majority of people—including many medical professionals—have viewed obesity as a matter of personal responsibility, resulting from individual choices such as eating too much food or not exercising enough. As a result, treatment has primarily consisted of urging the obese to change their behavior. However, this type of diagnosis and treatment has clearly been ineffective, because obesity rates have risen sharply in recent years.

In 2013 the American Medical Association (AMA) finally recognized that the medical community had been taking the wrong approach and officially recognized obesity as a disease. The organization explains that like other diseases, obesity is not simply a matter of personal choice. Rather, it is a medical condition in which the body does not function as it should. The AMA insists, "There is now an overabundance of clinical evidence to identify obesity as a multi-metabolic and hormonal disease state."[34] While some people continue to argue that responsibility for obesity falls on the individual, an increasing number of experts are following the AMA's lead and recognizing that in reality, a person's weight is heavily influenced by many other factors that are beyond personal control.

Genetics

A person's weight is strongly influenced by the genes he or she was born with. To understand the role genetics plays in obesity and other health issues, researchers often study twins or members of the same family, because these people share many genes. Such research has revealed evidence that genetics significantly influences a person's BMI and risk of obesity. For example, numerous twin studies have shown that identical twins are likely to have similar BMIs, even when they have different diet and exercise habits. For this reason, the Obesity Care Continuum insists, "it is evident that obesity is not a simple matter of choice."[35] Instead, the organization reports that family studies have shown that about 50 percent of the risk of obesity can be inherited.

> "Instead of dying from challenges against which our bodies were designed to protect us, we're now more likely to die from the protective traits themselves."[36]
>
> —Lee Goldman, a cardiologist and chief executive of Columbia University Medical Center

Not only do some people have genes that make them more likely to become obese, but researchers believe that the human race in general is genetically programmed to overeat when food is plentiful. This is because for thousands of years, humans lived a hunter-gatherer lifestyle, in which they had to actively look for food every day. They always faced the threat of starvation, so in times when food was plentiful, they ate a lot in order to store energy. Eating like this was an essential survival trait.

Community Layout Affects Obesity and Diabetes

Many people become obese because they live in communities that are not designed to encourage physical activity. In 2014 and 2015, Gallup studied forty-eight communities across the United States to better understand whether a community's layout affects the likelihood of its residents having active lifestyles. Gallup found that communities that support active lifestyles —by providing parks and bike trails, for example—did indeed have lower rates of both obesity and diabetes. This indicates that obesity can be a matter of where one lives, rather than willpower or personal responsibility.

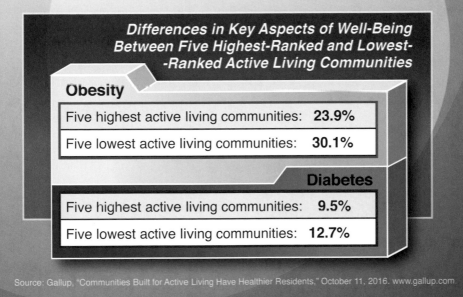

Differences in Key Aspects of Well-Being Between Five Highest-Ranked and Lowest--Ranked Active Living Communities

Obesity

Five highest active living communities:	23.9%
Five lowest active living communities:	30.1%

Diabetes

Five highest active living communities:	9.5%
Five lowest active living communities:	12.7%

Source: Gallup, "Communities Built for Active Living Have Healthier Residents," October 11, 2016. www.gallup.com.

However, over time humans have learned how to grow and distribute food in a system that makes it plentiful and relatively inexpensive for most people. Cardiologist Lee Goldman says that this is good news because it has helped life expectancy increase dramatically. However, humans are still genetically programmed to eat as much as they can when food is plentiful, and in modern society that is all the time. As a result, Goldman says, "instead of dying from challenges against which our bodies were designed to protect us, we're now more likely to die from the protective traits themselves."[36]

Strong Environmental Forces

In addition to genes, there are strong environmental forces encouraging people to consume too many calories and exercise too little. The government website Let's Move! explains that the environment has changed in the past thirty years, especially for young people, and many of these changes make obesity more likely. For example, in the past children usually walked to school, participated in gym class, ran around at recess, and played after school. In addition, home-cooked meals were relatively small, and both fast food and snacking were rare. All of these habits helped keep them at a healthy weight.

In contrast, young people live differently today. "Walks to and from school have been replaced by car and bus rides," Let's Move! reports. "Gym class and after-school sports have been cut; afternoons are now spent with TV, video games, and the internet. Parents are busier than ever and families eat fewer home-cooked meals. Snacking between meals is now commonplace."[37] All of these factors encourage young people to eat more and exercise less, making obesity more likely.

Obesity might also be the result of many Americans living in what are known as food deserts, or neighborhoods that lack easy access to healthy food such as fresh fruits and vegetables. In 2010 the US government estimated that about 23.5 million Americans faced this problem. "I live in one of those food deserts," says Jennifer Harris of the Rudd Center for Food Policy & Obesity. "The closest supermarket is 2.7 miles away and on a different bus line. If I didn't have a car, it would take me more than one hour each way to reach those 'fruit and vegetables from around the world.'"[38] As a result of having limited access to healthy foods, many people eat less healthy options such as fast food, which has more calories and can promote obesity.

> "I live in one of those food deserts. The closest supermarket is 2.7 miles away and on a different bus line. If I didn't have a car, it would take me more than one hour each way."[38]
>
> —Jennifer Harris, Director of Marketing Initiatives at the Rudd Center for Food Policy & Obesity

Chemicals and Bacteria Play a Role

There is also evidence that obesity may be a result of chemical changes to the human body. It is argued that some environmental chemicals—often referred to as obesogens—act like hormones. They can change the normal functioning of the body, making individuals more likely to become obese regardless of what they eat or how much they exercise. Obesogenic chemicals are used to make many everyday products, including cosmetics, shampoos, furniture, and foods. One example of an obesogen is bisphenol A (BPA). Researchers have found a connection between exposure to BPA and a number of health problems, including obesity. Anna Bellisari, author of *The Anthropology of Obesity in the United States*, explains how pervasive this chemical is. "It is found in baby bottles, reusable water bottles, sports equipment, eyeglasses, CDs, medical devices, coatings of food and beverage cans, water pipes, dental sealants, paints, papers, cardboards, cigarette filters, and American banknotes."[39] BPA is just one of numerous suspected obesogens that are pervasive in the modern environment.

Another theory about what is causing rising obesity levels involves bacteria in the human digestive system. Via a number of studies conducted on animals, researchers have found significant differences between the bacteria in the intestines of obese animals and those in animals of normal weight. They think these differences play a role in whether the animals gain weight. Gastroenterologist Gerard Mullin explains of one study:

> In genetically engineered obese mice, scientists found a class of gut microbes called Firmicutes was consistently overrepresented. They discovered that the Firmicutes are too efficient at extracting energy from food, breaking down fiber and even increasing the absorption of dietary fat. In this way, gut microbes could cause retention of body weight without the animal eating an extra morsel of food.[40]

Researchers believe that these findings are not limited to animals; humans are also more or less likely to become obese depending on the type of bacteria found in their intestines.

More than Just Choice

Overall, the evidence shows that obesity is caused by factors beyond individual choices about diet and exercise. Epidemiologist and medical doctor Deborah A. Cohen points out that people who are overweight seem to be able to exert a reasonable amount of control over other aspects of their lives. "They have completed school and earned college or higher degrees; they maintain full- or part-time jobs, arrive at work on time, complete their assignments, raise successful children, vote, volunteer, and contribute to society in many ways," she says. "Few get into trouble with the law or are violent, impulsive, or irresponsible in ways that demonstrate low self-control."[41] Given this, it seems unlikely that when it comes to weight, these same people are unable to exert control over their appetites. The likely reason is that obesity is not due to a lack of personal responsibility but is rather the result of profound genetic and environmental forces.

Chapter Three

Is the Food Industry to Blame for Obesity?

The Food Industry Is to Blame for Obesity

- The food industry creates foods that encourage overeating.
- Restaurants and food manufacturers offer large portion sizes that make people eat more.
- Powerful marketing campaigns make obesity more likely.

The Debate at a Glance

The Food Industry Is Not to Blame for Obesity

- There is no evidence that eating fast food causes people to become obese.
- Food manufacturers offer consumers a variety of choices, and obesity results when consumers make poor ones.
- Consumers frequently demand unhealthy food and refuse healthy options.

The Food Industry Is to Blame for Obesity

"Restaurateurs and purveyors of food need to be held responsible for what they serve. The amount of food we eat depends on the conditions in which it is served and sold. If the food industry wasn't selling us so much food that makes us sick, we wouldn't be sick."

—Deborah A. Cohen, an epidemiologist and medical doctor

Deborah A. Cohen, *A Big Fat Crisis*. New York: Nation, 2014, p. 198.

Consider these questions as you read:

1. Do you think obesity rates would be affected if Americans became more involved in growing and preparing their own food? If so, why? If not, why not?
2. In your experience, do foods with a lot of fat, sugar, and salt lead to overeating? Give an example.
3. Thinking about the facts and ideas presented in this essay, how persuasive is the argument that the food industry is to blame for obesity? Which arguments are strongest and why? Which arguments are weakest and why?

Editor's note: The discussion that follows presents common arguments made in support of this perspective, reinforced by facts, quotes, and examples taken from various sources.

Americans have become further and further removed from the food they eat. One hundred years ago, almost all meals were prepared at home from scratch, and about half of the population actually lived and worked on the farms that grew many of their ingredients. Now, only about 2 percent of Americans are farmers, and many people purchase foods that have already been prepared for them by manufacturers or restaurants. In fact, according to a 2011 report by the Organisation for Economic Co-operation and Development, Americans only spend about thirty minutes cooking per day. Instead, they rely on huge corporations to grow, process, and prepare ready-to-eat foods, which they then buy at grocery stores or restaurants. "From our agricultural lands to our mouths, our daily food is shaped, controlled, and marketed by commercial interests," notes food policy expert James E. Tillotson. "What these commercial interests offer is what Americans largely eat and drink; we have few other options."[42] This food industry is extremely powerful and a major cause of the obesity epidemic.

Making Food That Encourages Overeating

The food industry contributes to obesity by way of what is in the food it creates. A large percentage of processed and fast food contains high levels of sugar, fat, and salt, and researchers have found that these ingredients actually cause people to overeat. Most people naturally want to eat when they are hungry, and they stop when they are full. However, foods with large amounts of sugar, fat, and salt cause the brain to release pleasurable chemicals, and as a result people want to keep eating more in order to feel good, even when they are full. "Instead of satisfying our hunger, these foods train our bodies and our brains to want more,"[43] explains David A. Kessler, former commissioner of the US Food and Drug Administration. Journalist Mika Brzezinski points out that in contrast, people rarely feel compelled to overeat more natural foods like nuts and fruit. "You don't see people stuffing themselves with fruits, vegetables, lean meats, and nuts," she says. "Have I ever sat down and eaten a supersize bowl of broccoli? No way! But like millions of Americans, I have polished off a big bag of potato chips or a pint of ice cream at one sitting."[44]

> "Instead of satisfying our hunger, these foods train our bodies and our brains to want more."[43]
>
> —David A. Kessler, former commissioner of the US Food and Drug Administration

Increased Portion Sizes Contribute to Obesity

This chart shows how portion sizes of soda and other foods have substantially increased since the 1970s. Research shows that when people are offered a larger serving of food, they are likely to eat more. If people are continually receiving bigger portions and eating more, this could be responsible for rising obesity rates.

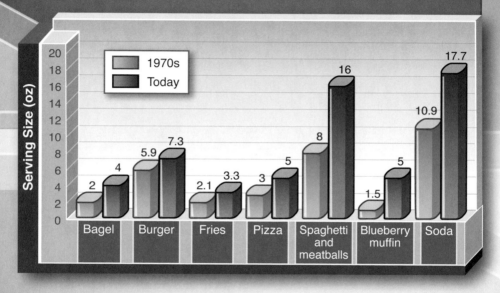

Source: Erin Brodwin and Samantha Lee, "Something We Have No Control Over Could Be Playing a Huge Role in Weight Gain," *Business Insider*, April 8, 2016. www.businessinsider.com.

In fact, companies specifically create foods high in fat, sugar, and salt precisely to get consumers to buy their products. "Food companies, including fast food chains, understand this [effect of these ingredients] very well," says Kessler. "They are hard at work to make new foods that will get us to keep eating."[45] As a result of an abundance of processed foods designed to make them keep eating, many Americans overeat all the time. To sell more items, food companies keep making these products salty, sweet, and with large amounts of fat, and consumers keep buying them because they taste so good. "If you ask food companies to make products that are much lower in sugar and salt, those products do very badly," explains nutritionist David Katz. "Nobody buys them. And then the food companies say, 'Hey, we tried, but we're not going to go out of business to make the public health types happy, so forget about it.'"[46]

Michael Prager, who formerly weighed 365 pounds (166 kg), knows just how compelling foods with lots of fat, sugar, and salt can be. His inability to reject these ingredients once caused him to eat three fast-food meals in a row. "I went through the drive-thru at the first place. I pulled over so I could eat in secret, although I'm fully aware that you can see through the windows of cars. Then I went next door to the next one. I bought another entire meal—soda, fries, sandwich—pulled over, ate it, and then I went to the next one and did the same thing. Three of them at one time."[47] Prager is not alone; millions of Americans find it difficult to say no to the addictive trifecta of fat, sugar, and salt.

This is in part because many modern products contain different types of ingredients than those in the past. For example, in the 1950s most of Americans' sugar intake came from natural sources like cane and beets. Today much of it comes in highly processed forms such as high fructose corn syrup and artificial sweeteners. Some research shows that these types of processed ingredients have a weight-gain effect different than their natural counterparts. For example, in 2010 a study by researchers at Princeton University found that rats that consumed high-fructose corn syrup gained significantly more weight than those that consumed table sugar, even when both consumed the same overall number of calories.

Increased Portion Sizes

The food industry also prompts consumers to eat more by serving large portions. Research shows that portion sizes of numerous foods have increased significantly in recent years. For instance, according to the CDC, hamburgers are three times bigger than they were in the 1950s, while the average restaurant meal is more than four times bigger than it was. Similarly, according to the National Institutes of Health, twenty years ago the typical bottle of soda was 6.5 ounces (192 ml), while today soda bottles are often 20 ounces (591 ml).

This contributes to obesity because when people receive larger portions of food, they tend to eat more overall. In fact, people have a natural instinct to choose and eat the largest portion available, because that is how their hunter-gatherer ancestors survived. "For our ancestors, it was easy—get the biggest portion you can find and eat it all before someone takes it away from you,"[48] explains cardiologist Lee Goldman of Columbia University Medical Center. An experiment in which moviegoers in a suburban Philadelphia theater were given free popcorn demonstrates just how strong this instinct still is. People were randomly selected to receive either a medium-size container or one that was twice as large. "People who received the larger container ate more popcorn than those who received the medium-size container—45 percent more when the popcorn was fresh and tasted good,"[49] says Goldman. Even when the popcorn was stale and tasted bad, moviegoers still ate one-third more of it when they received the large container, showing just how influential portion size can be.

> "People who received the larger container ate more popcorn than those who received the medium-size container—45 percent more when the popcorn was fresh and tasted good."[49]
>
> —Lee Goldman, a cardiologist

Powerful Marketing

The food industry also contributes to obesity by aggressively pursuing consumers—especially children—with powerful marketing campaigns that further increase their likelihood of eating a particular food. Consider the thought that goes into how foods are placed in a supermarket. When people enter, they are immediately confronted with displays of inexpensive and unhealthy foods like chips and cookies, which are placed at the ends of the aisles. Epidemiologist Deborah A. Cohen explains that vendors often pay supermarkets to display their products in these places, because research shows people are much more likely to buy items in these areas. "In fact, supermarkets now make more money selling their shelf space to vendors than they do selling their products to customers,"[50] says Cohen.

Children in particular are exposed to a lot of advertising for unhealthy food, and many worry this is among the reasons why obesity rates have risen among that age group. According to a report by the Rudd Center for Food Policy & Obesity, in 2015 children viewed an average of almost twelve food-related ads each day, and adolescents viewed about thirteen. Researchers found that three-quarters of the ads were for candy, cereals, snacks, or fast-food restaurants. The authors of *Childhood Obesity* stress, "The diet advertised to children stands in marked contrast with recommended guidelines on healthy nutrition."[51] While many other countries restrict how food and beverages are advertised to children, the United States has no such restrictions.

For these reasons and more, powerful food and beverage companies are a major contributing factor to the global problem of obesity. "A powerful corporation can sell the public just about anything," warns Margaret Chan, director-general of WHO. "Not one single country has managed to turn around its obesity epidemic in all age groups. This is not a failure of individual willpower. This is a failure of political will to take on big business."[52] As long as the food industry continues to exert such power, it will be very difficult to prevent obesity.

The Food Industry Is Not to Blame for Obesity

"It's not fair to demonize the food industry. It has done a lot of good by providing a greater variety of safer food to more people for lower prices. We must share the responsibility for their shortcomings, because their less healthy offerings were created in response to public demand."

—Harriet Hall, writer for *Science-Based Medicine*

Harriet Hall, "Does the Movie *Fed Up* Make Sense?," *Science-Based Medicine* (blog), October 14, 2014. www.sciencebasedmedicine.org.

Consider these questions as you read:

1. John Cisna lost 56 pounds (25 kg) by eating only at McDonald's for six months. Do you think his experience proves the fast-food industry is not to blame for obesity? Why or why not?
2. Do you agree that many consumers demand unhealthy food from the food industry and refuse to purchase healthier options? Why or why not?
3. Mike, the personal trainer discussed in the essay, suggests that food quantity, not quality, more significantly contributes to obesity. Do you agree? If so, why? If not, why not?

Editor's note: The discussion that follows presents common arguments made in support of this perspective, reinforced by facts, quotes, and examples taken from various sources.

On September 15, 2013, Iowa high school science teacher John Cisna began a six-month-long experiment in which he ate all of his meals at McDonald's. He wanted to prove that the fast-food chain is not responsible for obesity. While Cisna only ate McDonald's food, he controlled what he ate, restricted his diet to two thousand calories a day, and followed the recommended daily allowances for carbohydrates, protein, fat, and sugar. In addition, he got exercise by walking for forty-five minutes a day. At the beginning of his experiment, Cisna weighed 280 pounds (127 kg) and was considered obese. But after six months on the McDonald's diet, he had lost 56 pounds (25 kg), had lower cholesterol levels than when he started, and had normal blood pressure and sodium levels.

> "We all have choices. It's our choices that make us fat, not McDonald's."[53]
>
> —John Cisna, high school science teacher

He created a documentary about his experiment in which he argues that it is not the food industry that makes people obese, but rather the choices individuals make about their diet and physical activity. "We all have choices," he says. "It's our choices that make us fat, not McDonald's."[53] Society often blames restaurants and manufacturers for obesity, but as Cisna's story illustrates, a person's weight is ultimately the result of his or her own actions, not the food industry's.

No Evidence That Fast Food Causes Obesity

McDonald's and other fast-food chains are often singled out as a cause of obesity because their menus typically contain many high-calorie items such as French fries. It's true that a Big Mac, medium fries, and medium soda will supply individuals with more than half of their daily calorie needs (based on a two thousand-calorie-a-day diet). But while it might seem logical that such calorie-dense food causes obesity, a number of research studies show no evidence that this is true.

For example, in a study published in 2014 in the *American Journal of Clinical Nutrition*, researchers analyzed the diets of 4,466 US children aged two to eighteen to better understand whether obesity is associated with fast-food consumption in particular, since fast food is often blamed for obesity. The researchers found it is not actually the consumption of fast food that causes obesity in children, but the food that makes up the remainder of their diet. A study by researchers David Just and Brian

No Relationship Between Fast-Food Consumption and BMI

In a study involving almost five thousand people, researchers found that for the majority of the population, there is no evidence linking fast-food consumption with higher BMI. The researchers excluded the extremely underweight and the extremely overweight from their sample—about 5 percent of those studied—and found that for the remaining 95 percent of the sample, there was no relationship between their BMI and how often they consumed fast food. Regardless of BMI, they consumed about the same number of fast-food meals per week.

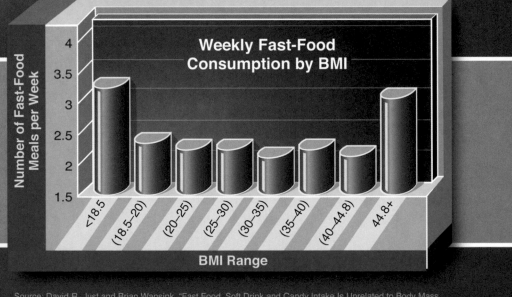

Weekly Fast-Food Consumption by BMI

Source: David R. Just and Brian Wansink, "Fast Food, Soft Drink and Candy Intake Is Unrelated to Body Mass Index for 95% of American Adults," *Obesity Science & Practice*, November 26, 2015. http://onlinelibrary.wiley.com.

Wansink, published in 2015 in *Obesity Science & Practice*, yielded a similar finding. The researchers looked at a sample of almost five thousand adults to understand how the consumption of unhealthy foods such as fast food and dessert was related to their BMI. The researchers excluded the extremely underweight (BMI <18.5) and the extremely overweight (BMI 44.8+) from the study—about 5 percent of the sample—and analyzed the other 95 percent. They found no relationship between BMI and the consumption of these foods. "If we want real change we need to look at the overall diet, and physical activity," concluded Just. "Narrowly targeting junk foods is not just ineffective, it may be self-defeating as it distracts from the real underlying causes of obesity."[54]

Quantity Not Quality

Mike is a personal trainer who knows just how ineffective it is to demonize fast and junk food. He has found that the quantity of what he eats is far more important to his weight than exactly what he eats. In fact, he became overweight while following a strict diet that banned junk food but was actually able to lose weight on a diet that *included* junk food. Mike reports that for six months he followed the Paleo diet, which focuses on eating natural foods such as animal protein, fruits, vegetables, nuts, and seeds and avoids all processed and junk foods. While the Paleo diet limited the types of food Mike could eat, it did not limit quantity. As a result, he found himself eating large amounts of unprocessed, healthy food but quickly becoming overweight. He eventually realized that simply avoiding certain products like junk food was not the path to his desired weight. "I realised that I'd been looking too much into supposed food 'quality' and not enough at food quantity," he says. Mike's new diet includes junk food. "I went on holiday to Amsterdam and Barcelona, and eyeballed all my food, eating Pop Tarts, burgers, pizza, pasta and sandwiches, and drinking beer and cocktails."[55] Because he limits the amount of what he eats, Mike is the leanest he has even been.

Consumers Have Choices—and What They Choose Is Telling

As Mike's story shows, consumers have many choices about what to eat—and how much. When people become obese, it is because of their choices—not because the food industry is forcing them to eat a certain way. In fact, food companies routinely manufacture multiple variations on a product—a lower-calorie version, one with low salt, ones that come in different package sizes—so consumers can choose exactly what they want. Food companies cannot be blamed if some consumers simply want the larger, higher-fat, or saltier versions. "Nearly all soft drink companies produce similar low-calorie, zero-calorie, and sugar-free varieties," points out Christopher Snowdon of the Institute of Economic Affairs. "All are widely advertised and all are available on the same shelves, in the same stores, and for the same price as their more sugary cousins." With so many options, "it is very difficult to argue that consumers are nudged, let alone coerced, into buying the high-calorie variants," says Snowdon. "If they buy them it is because they want them."[56]

> "It is very difficult to argue that consumers are nudged, let alone coerced, into buying the high-calorie variants. If they buy them it is because they want them."[56]
>
> —Christopher Snowdon, director of Lifestyle Economics at the Institute of Economic Affairs

The fact is that when it comes to sodas—and food in general—consumers often want the higher-calorie options and frequently refuse to buy healthier alternatives. McDonald's McLean Deluxe burger is an excellent example of the fact that when the industry offers a healthier option, many people reject it. The McLean Deluxe was introduced in 1991, and McDonald's praised it as a healthier, reduced-fat menu choice. However, it turned out that consumers did not *want* a healthier burger, and the McLean Deluxe was a huge failure. "The general reaction varied from lack of interest to mockery to revulsion," explains journalist David H. Freedman. "The company gamely flogged the sandwich for five years before quietly removing it from the menu."[57]

In fact, Freedman argues that many consumers are so strongly opposed to choosing healthy options that, in order to successfully sell them, manufacturers have to be sneaky about it. "While the company has heavily plugged the debut of its new egg-white sandwich and chicken wraps, the ads have left out even a mention of health, the reduced calories and fat, or the inclusion of whole grains," says Freedman about new, healthier items on McDonald's menu. "McDonald's has practically kept secret the fact that it has also begun substituting whole-grain flour for some of the less healthy refined flour in its best-selling Egg McMuffin."[58] Amazingly, the company has to minimize mention of health or consumers will not want to buy its food.

Overall, few Americans agree that the food industry is to blame for obesity. In a study published in *Appetite* in 2013, Brenna Ellison and Jayson Lusk surveyed eight hundred people on who is to blame for obesity. Respondents evaluated the role of grocery stores, farmers, restaurants, food manufacturers, individuals, parents, and even the government. They overwhelmingly blamed individuals—80 percent of those surveyed said individuals are responsible for the rise in obesity, not the food industry. The food industry is simply doing its job—to create a variety of products and offer them all to the consumer. If people continually choose the unhealthiest options, the blame would seem to lie with them.

Chapter Four

Can the United States Reduce the Problem of Obesity?

The United States Can Reduce the Problem of Obesity

- The government can and should regulate the food industry to help reduce obesity.
- Obesity can be reduced by making diet and exercise changes.
- Bariatric surgery is an effective solution to obesity.
- Taking obesity drugs is an effective way to lose weight.

The Debate at a Glance

The United States Cannot Reduce the Problem of Obesity

- Diet and exercise usually fail to reduce obesity.
- Weight-loss drugs do not cause significant weight loss for most people.
- Bariatric surgery often fails to provide lasting results.
- Government regulation to reduce obesity has proved ineffective.

The United States Can Reduce the Problem of Obesity

"America, we have a weight problem. But don't despair, we can beat it. We have faced other challenges as a nation, and we can overcome this one."

—Francis Collins, director of the National Institutes of Health

Quoted in Nanci Hellmich, "To Fight Obesity, USA Needs a Plan," *USA Today*, November 5, 2012. www.usatoday.com.

Consider these questions as you read:

1. In Japan adults age forty and older have their waistlines measured every year. Do you think Americans would agree to a similar requirement? Why or why not?

2. Do you think taxing soda is an effective way to reduce its consumption? Why or why not?

3. Given what you know on this topic, how strong is the argument that people can fight obesity through diet and exercise changes? Explain your reasoning.

Editor's note: The discussion that follows presents common arguments made in support of this perspective, reinforced by facts, quotes, and examples taken from various sources.

Less than 4 percent of Japan's population is obese, which is very low compared to most other countries. Experts believe a reason why is that the Japanese government has actively sought to prevent obesity among its citizens. For instance, in 2008 it passed a law that requires adults aged forty to seventy-four to have their waistlines measured each year. Men whose waistlines exceed 33.5 inches (85 cm) and women whose exceed

35.4 inches (90 cm) are required to lose weight or receive dietary counseling. In addition, companies and local governments whose members fail to meet certain weight-related goals must pay fines. Japan is proof that it is possible for a country to effectively prevent obesity. The United States has a much higher obesity rate than Japan—one of the highest in the world—but like Japan, it could take action to successfully reduce its problem.

Government Regulation

The first step in the fight against obesity is for the US government to take a much more active role in the problem. Indeed, obesity is a public health problem that needs to be addressed by the government, just as the government addresses other threats to public health, such as environmental pollution or food-borne illness. The public has accepted government regulation in numerous other areas and would be likely to do so regarding obesity. "In all industries, in all worksites, and for all consumer goods, we have accepted the role of government to discourage practices that increase the risk of unhealthy outcomes, be it unintended injury or long-term disabling disease,"[59] notes epidemiologist Deborah A. Cohen. However, when it comes to food, the government has largely taken the position that industry is free to manufacture and market whatever products it wants, and individuals are free to make their own choices about what to eat. This is not in the best interest of the American public, nor does the United States follow this policy in other areas. For example, seat belts and airbags in cars are not a matter of personal choice but are mandated by the government because there is strong evidence that they significantly improve public safety. The food industry should similarly be subject to greater regulation as a matter of public safety.

> "In all industries, in all worksites, and for all consumer goods, we have accepted the role of government to discourage practices that increase the risk of unhealthy outcomes, be it unintended injury or long-term disabling disease."[59]
>
> —Deborah A. Cohen, an epidemiologist and medical doctor

Bariatric Surgery Reduces the Risk of Death from Obesity

Research shows that bariatric surgery can be an effective way to reduce deaths resulting from obesity-related health problems. This graph shows the results of a study that compared the death rates of 2,500 obese people who had bariatric surgery with the death rates of 7,462 obese patients who did not have the surgery. The people who underwent surgery had a significantly lower chance of dying in the years following their surgeries.

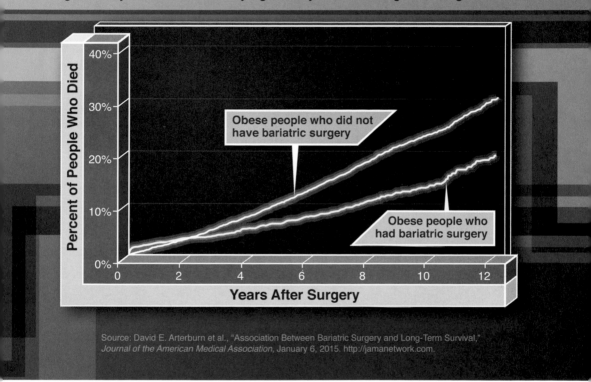

Source: David E. Arterburn et al., "Association Between Bariatric Surgery and Long-Term Survival," *Journal of the American Medical Association*, January 6, 2015. http://jamanetwork.com.

One way the government could intervene to reduce obesity is by introducing a soda tax. Many Americans drink soda every day, yet it contains large amounts of sugar. In fact, nutrition expert Marion Nestle reports that sugary drinks account for half of all the sugar that is consumed in the United States. Soda consumption is a primary reason for increasing obesity rates, and taxing it would incentivize people to drink less of it and thus trigger weight loss. "Many people can lose weight, keep it off, and reduce or eliminate symptoms of diabetes by doing nothing more than removing sugary drinks from their daily diets,"[60] says Nestle. In 2012 the Rudd Center for Food Policy & Obesity reported that a 10 percent increase in the price of soda would decrease consumption by an estimated 8 percent to 12.6 percent. In addition to reducing consumption, revenue from the tax could be used to fund other obesity prevention and treatment efforts. Indeed, this has been a successful model for antismoking efforts—extra taxes on cigarettes reduce consumption and help pay for antismoking campaigns.

Another effective government intervention would be to mandate that schools teach healthy habits so that children learn to maintain a healthy weight at the onset of their lives. This is important, because it is much easier to address obesity before it happens than afterward. As pediatrician Susan Prescott stresses, "Prevention must be the ultimate approach."[61] Since children spend a large portion of their time in school, teachers have a lot of opportunity to influence them to make healthy choices. The government should further ensure that schools provide children with healthy lunches, educate them about nutrition, and encourage them to be physically active. Because they are not currently required to do most of these things, many schools have moved in the opposite direction, cutting back on physical education (PE) and eliminating nutrition classes. For instance, according to the 2016 report *Shape of the Nation*, which examined the state of PE in the United States, only Oregon and the District of Columbia meet the national recommendation for PE time for both elementary and middle schools.

Diet and Exercise Changes

Physical education and diet are also an important part of reducing obesity. Research shows the majority of Americans consume too many calories and do not get enough exercise, both of which contribute to high obesity rates. The nation could dramatically decrease these rates if Americans simply changed their habits. Helen Darling, president and CEO of the National Business Group on Health, explains there is a simple formula to preventing obesity: "Eat the number of nutritionally dense calories every day that balances the amount of calories you burn each day, and you will not gain weight. It really is as simple as that."[62] Unfortunately, most people are not doing this. "The sheer volume of food consumed by the average American is striking, with the typical adult eating 2,700 calories per day," according to David Blumenthal, president and CEO of the Commonwealth Fund, a national health care philanthropy group. "This vastly exceeds the healthy level for a majority of the population."[63] Research also shows a striking deficit in physical exercise. According to the CDC's 2015 Youth Risk Behavior Survey of high school students, less than half had been physically active for sixty minutes or more on five or more days a week, the amount recommended by health experts.

Medical Interventions

When a person has a significant amount of weight to lose, bariatric surgery can be an effective solution. In this type of surgery, doctors reduce the size of the stomach so as to limit the amount of food a person can eat and/or to reroute the small intestine so the body does not absorb as much food. According to the American Society for Metabolic and Bariatric Surgery, most patients successfully lose 50 percent or more of their excess body weight after bariatric surgery and manage to maintain that loss over the long term. "Such massive and sustained weight reduction with surgery is in sharp contrast to the experience most patients have previously had with non-surgical therapies,"[64] says the society.

Sixteen-year-old Shaina had bariatric surgery after she started to suffer vision loss from pressure on her optic nerve resulting from the fact that she was obese. She weighed 242 pounds (110 kg), and even though she was able to lose some weight on her own, she needed to lose more weight, and more quickly, in order to preserve her vision. Just three months after surgery, she was down to 184 pounds (83 kg), going from a size 20 to a 12. "I had to get a whole new wardrobe,"[65] she says.

Weight-loss drugs can also help combat obesity. The Mayo Clinic reports that when combined with diet and exercise, weight-loss drugs can help a person lose 5 percent to 10 percent of their total body weight within a year. While this may seem like a modest amount of weight, even this level of change can significantly improve a person's health. Experts believe that scientists will create even more effective weight-loss drugs in the future and that these will play an increasingly important role in the fight against obesity.

Overall, there are many ways the United States can reduce its national problem of obesity. CDC Director Thomas Frieden is among many who believe that communities should be determined to find various solutions and adopt the best ones. If US communities make a purposeful and determined effort, he says, "I am very confident we can reverse the obesity epidemic."[66]

> "I am very confident we can reverse the obesity epidemic."[66]
>
> —Thomas Frieden, director of the CDC

The United States Cannot Reduce the Problem of Obesity

"It is clear the United States is facing a rising obesity problem. But the challenge remains: We have yet to determine a successful way to tackle it."

—Sherzod Abdukadirov and Michael Marlow of the Mercatus Center at George Mason University

Sherzod Abdukadirov and Michael Marlow, "Government Intervention Will Not Solve Our Obesity Problem," *U.S. News & World Report*, June 5, 2012. www.usnews.com.

Consider these questions as you read:

1. Why is bariatric surgery not always an effective long-term solution? What might help it become so? Explain your answer.
2. In your opinion, is it the job of the government to try to reduce obesity among the citizenry? Why or why not?
3. Do you agree that most Americans have a higher quality of life than they did fifty years ago, even if they are obese? Why or why not?

Editor's note: The discussion that follows presents common arguments made in support of this perspective, reinforced by facts, quotes, and examples taken from various sources.

Tara Parker-Pope writes the *Well* blog for the *New York Times*. Despite knowing a lot about health and weight, and despite working very hard to keep her weight down, she has struggled with it for much of her life. She says:

> I have always felt perplexed about my inability to keep weight off. I know the medical benefits of weight loss, and I don't drink sugary sodas or eat fast food. I exercise regularly—a few years ago, I even completed a marathon. Yet during the 23 years since

graduating from college, I've lost 10 or 20 pounds at a time, maintained it for a little while and then gained it all back and more, to the point where I am now easily 60 pounds overweight.[67]

Stories like Parker-Pope's are the rule, not the exception. Obesity researcher Rudolph Leibel insists that until they actually try it, many people do not understand just how difficult it is to combat obesity. He says. "We don't want to make [obese people] feel hopeless, but we do want to make them understand that they are trying to buck a biological system that is going to make it hard for them."[68] The fact is that obesity has become a part of modern society, and the United States will not be able to reduce this problem.

The United States Will Not Reduce Obesity Enough to Meet WHO Targets

Concerned by growing waistbands and related health problems, in 2011 the World Health Organization (WHO) set targets to reduce obesity and diabetes. By 2025, its goal is for obesity and diabetes rates to not increase higher than they were in 2010. According to analysis by the organization NCD Risk Factor Collaboration, however, the United States is likely to fail on both counts.

	Projection for 2025		Probability of meeting the global target	
	Men	Women	Men	Women
Obesity	45%	43%	0%	0%
Diabetes	9.9%	7.6%	32%	36%

Source: NCD Risk Factor Collaboration, "Country Profile: USA," 2016. www.ncdrisc.org.

No Easy Solution

The most commonly proposed solution to obesity is to get people to eat more healthfully and to exercise more. However, there is widespread evidence that simply modifying one's diet and exercise routine is not a successful long-term solution to obesity. Numerous studies show that people who are obese often fail to successfully lose weight by dieting and exercising. Even when they do manage to lose weight, they usually regain it within a few years. This is because while diet and exercise might be effective for someone who has never been obese, once a person has become obese, his or her body works hard to stay that way; it is thus extremely difficult to simply lose weight through diet and exercise.

Writing in the *Lancet* in 2015, researchers explain: "Once obesity is established . . . bodyweight seems to become biologically stamped in and defended."[69] They say the more weight a person loses, the harder his or her body tries to return back to his or her all-time highest weight. This disturbs researcher Christopher N. Ochner, who says, "What really

> "Weight-loss drugs have thus brought little aggregate benefit so far."[72]
>
> —Robert Paarlberg, political science professor

bothers me working around and with clinicians, is that some of them—a disturbing percentage—still believe it's all about personal choice: that if the patient just tries hard enough, and if we can just figure out how to get them a little more motivated, then we'd be successful. And that's just not right."[70] He insists that a person cannot combat obesity simply by trying to eat less and move more.

Others believe that weight-loss drugs are the solution to obesity. However, the majority of people who take such drugs fail to experience a significant benefit. There simply is no magic pill that can make people lose weight. "Every time a new drug hits the market, hope seems to fizzle into hype," says science journalist Carina Storrs. "The treatments—some pills and others injectables—are often long on limitations and side effects and, patients complain, short on effectiveness."[71] Robert Paarlberg, a member of the International Food Policy Research Institute and the United Nations' Food and Agriculture Organization, agrees. "On balance, weight-loss drugs have thus brought little aggregate benefit so far,"[72] he says. In addition, very few weight-loss drugs are approved for long-term use, their benefits tend to be fairly small, and the drugs are often very expensive. As a result, few obese Americans use them. Overall, Paarlberg estimates that only about 2 million out of 70 million obese Americans take prescribed weight-loss drugs.

There has been more short-term success with bariatric surgery, where doctors change the stomach and intestine so a person is forced to eat less or cannot absorb as many calories from food. However, while bariatric surgery can help a patient lose a lot of weight very quickly, it is not a long-term solution to keeping that weight off. Many patients eventually regain the weight by failing to follow their postsurgery diet and exercise recommendations. By consistently overeating, individuals can gradually stretch out their surgically altered stomach so they can eat large meals again. This happened to Denise, who after bariatric surgery went from being 300 pounds (136 kg) to 160 pounds (73 kg). However, she was unable to stay at her new weight for long. "After 5 years all my old habits gradually came back," she says. "I am back to eating until I am sick, eating when not hungry, eating fast food, following different diet plans for a week or two and then falling off the wagon and gaining what I lost plus some. EVERYTHING I did prior to weight loss surgery!"[73] After visiting her surgeon, she learned that her stomach had indeed stretched out again.

Regulatory Action

Since diet, exercise, and even surgery often fail to control obesity, some argue that government regulation is needed. However, numerous examples reveal that regulation is as ineffective as these other so-called solutions. For instance, some argue that taxing sodas and other sugary beverages can reduce the problem. However, research shows that such policies fail to deter consumption—a few cents more in the form of a tax is not enough to prevent people from drinking sugary drinks if they want to. "Interestingly, soda taxes mostly cause people without weight problems to cut back their consumption, even though they are not the intended targets of the policy," report Michael Marlow and Sherzod Abdukadirov from the Mercatus Center at George Mason University. "Meanwhile, frequent soda drinkers buy lower-priced soda, engage in bulk discounted purchases, and brew more sweetened ice tea."[74]

Government regulation in schools has also been unsuccessful. In an attempt to reduce obesity, schools in the United States and around the world have been forced to serve more healthy school lunches and to reduce the availability of junk food. However, a number of studies show that regulating school food does not seem to impact obesity rates. For example, in 2012 researchers from Pennsylvania State University looked at more than nineteen thousand middle-school-age children. They compared students in schools where junk food was sold with schools where it was not. They found no correlation between a student attending a school where junk food was available and obesity. This is largely because school represents just a small part of young people's food choices. "They can get food at home, they can get food in their neighborhoods, and they can go across the street from the school to buy food,"[75] said lead researcher Jennifer Van Hook. In another study, researchers from the Harvard School of Public Health found that when young people are given healthy food for school lunches, they often throw away that part of their meal—approximately 60 percent of their vegetables and 40 percent of their fruits. Few images can illustrate the futility of a health-promoting regulation better than a garbage can full of fruits and vegetables.

> "Interestingly, soda taxes mostly cause people without weight problems to cut back their consumption, even though they are not the intended targets of the policy."[74]
>
> —Sherzod Abdukadirov and Michael Marlow, senior scholar and research fellow, respectively, at the Mercatus Center at George Mason University

Obesity is a side effect of the modern lifestyle, and it is impossible to eliminate obesity without overhauling the entire lifestyle. Not only is that impossible to do, but maybe we should not try—while the modern lifestyle has led to higher obesity rates, it has also led to a better quality of life. "In the early 1970s, obesity prevalence in America was still below 15 percent," notes Paarlberg. "But this was made possible by higher physical labor requirements both at work and at home, less consumer purchasing power, more expensive food, more cigarette smoking, no microwave ovens, no personal computers, and less freedom for women to work outside the home."[76] If returning to any of these situations is the only way to reverse obesity, perhaps we are better off big. The United States would be wiser to recognize that obesity is simply part of modern life and cannot be reduced.

Source Notes

Overview: Obesity

1. Allyn L. Taylor and Michael F. Jacobson, "Carbonating the World: The Marketing and Health Impact of Sugar Drinks in Low- and Middle-Income Countries," Center for Science in the Public Interest, February 9, 2016. https://cspinet.org.
2. Robert Paarlberg, *The United States of Excess: Gluttony and the Dark Side of American Exceptionalism.* New York: Oxford University Press, 2015, p. 175.
3. Ping Zhang, Sundar S. Shrestha, and Rui Li, "Economic Costs of Obesity," in *Handbook of Obesity: Epidemiology, Etiology, and Physiopathology,* ed. George A. Bray and Claude Bouchard. Boca Raton, FL: CRC, 2014, p. 497.
4. John Hoffman, Judith A. Salerno, and Alexandra Moss, *The Weight of the Nation: To Win We Have to Lose.* New York: St. Martin's, 2012, p. 1.

Chapter One: Does Obesity Pose a Serious Health Threat?

5. Mirna Ortiz, "One Patient's Story: My Type 2 Diabetes," *Thriving* (blog), Boston Children's Hospital, December 18, 2009. https://thriving.children shospital.org.
6. Centers for Disease Control and Prevention, "Diabetes 2014 Report Card," 2014. www.cdc.gov.
7. psinguine, comment on AskReddit, "(Serious) Obese People of Reddit, What Is One of the Worst Daily Struggles You Face That 'Average' Sized People Wouldn't Know/Understand?," 2014. www.reddit.com.
8. Obese_won_Kenobi, comment on AskReddit, "(Serious) Obese People of Reddit, What Is One of the Worst Daily Struggles You Face That 'Average' Sized People Wouldn't Know/Understand?"
9. GregSchwall, comment on AskReddit, "(Serious) Obese People of Reddit, What Is One of the Worst Daily Struggles You Face That 'Average' Sized People Wouldn't Know/Understand?"
10. Rebecca Puhl, "Childhood Obesity and Stigma," Obesity Action Coalition, 2016. www.obesityaction.org.
11. Obesity Action Coalition, "Understanding Obesity Stigma," 2015. www .obesityaction.org.
12. Robert H. Lustig, *Fat Chance: Beating the Odds Against Sugar, Processed Food, Obesity, and Disease.* New York: Hudson Street, 2012, p. 6.
13. Jeffrey Levi et al., "The State of Obesity 2015: Better Policies for a Healthier America," State of Obesity, September 2015. http://stateofobesity.org.

14. Mission: Readiness, "Too Fat to Fight," 2010. https://strongnation.s3.amaz onaws.com.
15. Helen Clark, "Tackling Obesity and Overweight," in *"To Save Humanity": What Matters Most for a Healthy Future*, ed. Julio Frenk and Steven J. Hoffman. New York: Oxford University Press, 2015, p. 79.
16. Quoted in Nicole Lyn Pesce, "Can You Be Fat and Fit? These Plus-Size Athletes Say Yes," *New York Daily News*, October 9, 2015. www.nydailynews.com.
17. Center for Consumer Freedom, "An Epidemic of Obesity Myths," 2005. http://obesitymyths.com.
18. Risa Lavizzo-Mourey, "RWJF Statement on Obesity Rate Data from the Centers for Disease Control and Prevention," Robert Wood Johnson Foundation, November 12, 2015. http://www.rwjf.org.
19. Nadeem Esmail and Patrick Basham, "Obesity in Canada: Overstated Problems, Misguided Policy Solutions," Fraser Institute, April 2014. www.fraserinstitute.org.
20. *Chattanooga (TN) Times Free Press*, "Obesity Is Worth Celebrating," January 5, 2013. www.timesfreepress.com.
21. Andrew Weil, "Obese but Healthy?," Weil Lifestyle, October 5, 2016. www.drweil.com.
22. Quoted in Peg Rosen, "Can You Be Fat but Fit?," *Fitness*, June 2013. www.fitnessmagazine.com.
23. Quoted in Rosen, "Can You Be Fat but Fit?"
24. Marilyn Wann, "Big Deal: You Can Be Fat and Fit," CNN, January 3, 2013. www.cnn.com.

Chapter Two: Is Obesity a Matter of Personal Responsibility?

25. Heidi Bond and Jenna Glatzer, *Who's the New Kid? How an Ordinary Mom Helped Her Daughter Overcome Childhood Obesity—and You Can Too!* Carol Stream, IL: Tyndale House, 2015, pp. 194–95.
26. Quoted in Gabrielle Olya, "Woman Intentionally Gains and Loses 42 Lbs. for Controversial TLC Documentary," *People*, January 4, 2015. www.people.com.
27. Harvard School of Public Health, "Physical Activity," 2016. www.hsph.harvard.edu.
28. World Health Organization, "Report of the Commission on Ending Childhood Obesity," 2016. http://www.who.int.
29. Debbie Gisonni, "10 Ways Parents Can Take Responsibility for Child Obesity," *Huffington Post*, January 22, 2013. www.huffingtonpost.com.
30. Quoted in Sarah Corapi, "Why It Takes More than a Grocery Store to Eliminate a 'Food Desert,'" *PBS NewsHour*, February 3, 2014. www.pbs.org.
31. Christopher Snowdon, "Can Public Policy Stop Obesity? The Slippery Slope of Food Regulations," *Cato Unbound*, January 27, 2015. www.cato-unbound.org.

32. Harvard School of Public Health, "Genes Are Not Destiny," 2016. www .hsph.harvard.edu.

33. Quoted in Mika Brzezinski and Diane Smith, *Obsessed: America's Food Addiction—and My Own.* New York: Weinstein, 2013, p. 107.

34. American Medical Association House of Delegates, "Resolution 420 (A-13): Recognition of Obesity as a Disease," NPR, June 19, 2013. http:// media.npr.org.

35. Obesity Care Continuum, "Obesity and Disability," Obesity Society, January 2015. www.obesity.org.

36. Lee Goldman, *Too Much of a Good Thing: How Four Key Survival Traits Are Now Killing Us.* New York: Little, Brown, 2015, p. 5.

37. Let's Move!, "Learn the Facts." www.letsmove.gov.

38. Jennifer Harris, "Welcome to the Obesogenic Environment," *Cato Unbound*, February 3, 2015. www.cato-unbound.org.

39. Anna Bellisari, *The Anthropology of Obesity in the United States.* New York: Routledge, 2016, p. 146.

40. Gerard Mullin, "Imbalances in Our Gut Flora Contribute to the Obesity Epidemic: How Do We Fix This?," Medical Daily, July 5, 2015. www.med icaldaily.com.

41. Deborah A. Cohen, *A Big Fat Crisis.* New York: Nation, 2014, pp. 6–7.

Chapter Three: Is the Food Industry to Blame for Obesity?

42. James E. Tillotson, "Role of Agriculture and the Food Industry in America's Obesity," in *Handbook of Obesity*, p. 425.

43. David A. Kessler, *Your Food Is Fooling You: How Your Brain Is Hijacked by Sugar, Fat, and Salt.* New York: Roaring Brook, 2013, p. 7.

44. Brzezinski and Smith, *Obsessed*, p. 8.

45. Kessler, *Your Food Is Fooling You*, p. 7.

46. Quoted in Brzezinski and Smith, *Obsessed*, p. 102.

47. Quoted in Brzezinski and Smith, *Obsessed*, pp. 94–95.

48. Goldman, *Too Much of a Good Thing*, p. 228.

49. Goldman, *Too Much of a Good Thing*, p. 228.

50. Cohen, *A Big Fat Crisis*, p. 81.

51. Kristin Voight, Stuart G. Nicholls, and Garrath Williams, *Childhood Obesity: Ethical and Policy Issues.* New York: Oxford University Press, 2014, p. 156.

52. Margaret Chan, "WHO Director-General Addresses Health Promotion Conference," World Health Organization, June 10, 2013. www.who.int.

53. Quoted in Mark Tauscheck, "Science Teacher Creates Documentary Based on McDonald's Diet," KCCI.com, January 3, 2014. www.kcci.com.

54. Quoted in Katherine Baildon, "Is Junk Food to Blame?," Food & Brand Lab, Cornell University, 2016. http://foodpsychology.cornell.edu.

55. Mike, "How 'Clean Eating' Made Me Fat, but Ice Cream and Subway Got Me Lean," *Healthy Living Heavy Lifting* (blog), March 23, 2014. www .healthylivingheavylifting.com.

56. Snowdon, "Can Public Policy Stop Obesity?"
57. David H. Freedman, "How Junk Food Can End Obesity," *Atlantic*, July/August 2013. www.theatlantic.com.
58. Freedman, "How Junk Food Can End Obesity."

Chapter Four: Can the United States Reduce the Problem of Obesity?

59. Cohen, *A Big Fat Crisis*, p. 111.
60. Marion Nestle, *Soda Politics: Taking on Big Soda (and Winning)*. New York: Oxford University Press, 2015, p. 1.
61. Susan Prescott, *Origins: Early-Life Solutions to the Modern Health Crisis*. Crawley, Western Australia: UWA, 2015, p. 19.
62. Quoted in *Wall Street Journal*, "The Experts: What's the One Dietary Change the Average American Should Make?," June 18, 2013. www.wsj.com.
63. Quoted in *Wall Street Journal*, "The Experts."
64. American Society for Metabolic and Bariatric Surgery, "Bariatric Surgery Misconceptions," 2016. https://asmbs.org.
65. Quoted in Anne Harding, "Surgery Is No Quick Fix for Obese Teens," CNN, June 22, 2011. www.cnn.com.
66. Quoted in Nanci Hellmich, "To Fight Obesity, USA Needs a Plan," *USA Today*, November 5, 2012. www.usatoday.com.
67. Tara Parker-Pope, "The Fat Trap," *New York Times*, December 28, 2011. www.nytimes.com.
68. Quoted in Parker-Pope, "The Fat Trap."
69. Christopher N. Ochner et al., "Treating Obesity Seriously: When Recommendations for Lifestyle Change Confront Biological Adaptations," *Lancet Diabetes and Endocrinology*, February 11, 2015. www.thelancet.com.
70. Quoted in Melissa Healy, "Diet and Exercise Alone Are No Cure for Obesity, Experts Say," *Los Angeles Times*, February 13, 2015. www.latimes.com.
71. Carina Storrs, "New Weight Loss Drugs, but No Magic Pill," CNN, July 8, 2015. www.cnn.com.
72. Paarlberg, *The United States of Excess*, p. 169.
73. Denise, "8 Years Post-Weight Loss Surgery and Out of Control!," Bariatric Surgery Source, 2016. www.bariatric-surgery-source.com.
74. Sherzod Abdukadirov and Michael Marlow, "Government Intervention Will Not Solve Our Obesity Problem," *U.S. News & World Report*, June 5, 2012. www.usnews.com.
75. Quoted in American Sociological Association, "Study Suggests Junk Food in Schools Doesn't Cause Weight Gain Among Children," press release, January 17, 2012. www.asanet.org.
76. Paarlberg, *The United States of Excess*, p. 28.

Obesity Facts

Number of People Affected

- Gallup reports that after leveling off in 2012–2013, the US obesity rate has again started to rise.
- The CDC reports that from 2013 to 2015, obesity rates among ninth to twelfth graders hardly changed, going from 13.7 percent to 13.9 percent.
- According to a report by the State of Obesity, a project of the Trust for America's Health and the Robert Wood Johnson Foundation, the average American weighs 24 pounds (11 kg) more than in 1960.
- The American Heart Association compares obesity rates in 1971–1974 with rates found in 2009–2010; it reports that obesity among children ages six to eleven increased from 4 percent to 18 percent.
- According to a 2016 report published by the Center for Science in the Public Interest, more than half of all the obese people in the world live in just ten countries: the United States, India, China, Brazil, Russia, Mexico, Egypt, Germany, Indonesia, and Pakistan.

Health Effects

- The CDC estimates that children who are overweight or obese when they are preschoolers are five times more likely to be overweight or obese as adults.
- According to the American Heart Association, every day in the United States 13 million children deal with the health and emotional effects of obesity.
- Gallup finds that obese adults are approximately 4.7 times more likely to be diabetic than adults of a normal weight.
- The Obesity Society estimates that diabetes and complications related to this illness cause more than two hundred thousand deaths each year in the United States.
- The World Obesity Federation estimates that BMI accounts for 20 percent of a person's risk of developing hypertension and coronary heart disease.

Reducing Obesity

- According to the CDC's 2015 Youth Risk Behavior Survey, 45.6 percent of students in grades nine to twelve are trying to lose weight.
- In a 2013 survey, banking company Credit Suisse surveyed 152 doctors around the world and found that 86 percent believe that government and health officials should do more to reduce sugar consumption.
- The National Institute of Diabetes and Digestive and Kidney Diseases reports that on average, people who have bariatric surgery lose 15 percent to 30 percent of their presurgery weight.

Possible Causes of Obesity

- In a 2016 report, WHO estimates that 81 percent of young people ages eleven to seventeen do not get enough exercise.
- The CDC reports that only about 20 percent of Americans over age eighteen meet the guidelines for physical and muscle-strengthening activity.
- According to the CDC, half of all US children do not have a community center, park, or sidewalk in their neighborhood, which makes it harder for them to be physically active.
- The CDC estimates that on a typical day, 80 percent of youth drink sugar-sweetened drinks.
- According to the Rudd Center for Food Policy & Obesity, from 2014 to 2015 food, beverage, and restaurant advertising that targeted children decreased by 8 percent, and ads targeting adolescents decreased by 14 percent.
- According to a 2013 report by Credit Suisse, the world's daily average consumption of high-fructose corn syrup and sugar is seventeen teaspoons per person per day.
- The Robert Wood Johnson Foundation estimates that the majority of children ages two to seventeen spend at least twenty hours a week watching television.

Related Organizations and Websites

Center for Science in the Public Interest (CSPI)
1220 L St. NW, Suite 300
Washington, DC 20005
website: https://cspinet.org

The CSPI seeks to create a healthier food system in the United States. It works to educate the public and counter the influence of the food industry on public policy and opinion. The organization publishes the *Nutrition Action Healthletter* and the website Nutrition Action.

Division of Nutrition, Physical Activity, and Obesity
Centers for Disease Control and Prevention (CDC)
1600 Clifton Rd.
Atlanta, GA 30329
website: www.cdc.gov/nccdphp/dnpao

The CDC's Division of Nutrition, Physical Activity, and Obesity promotes healthy eating and active living as a way to keep Americans healthy. It works to increase healthy food choices and help people find places where they can be physically active. Its website contains statistics, maps, reports, and fact sheets about obesity.

Let's Move!
website: www.letsmove.gov

Let's Move! is an initiative launched by Michelle Obama as First Lady of the United States. It is dedicated to solving the problem of obesity within a generation. To do so, it works to promote access to healthy foods and encourages children to be physically active. Its website offers information about obesity and how to prevent and reduce it.

National Association to Advance Fat Acceptance (NAAFA)
PO Box 4662
Foster City, CA 94404
website: www.naafaonline.com

The NAAFA is a nonprofit civil rights organization that works to protect the quality of life for overweight people. It believes that discrimination based on body size is wrong and aims to provide overweight people with tools for self-empowerment.

Obesity Action Coalition (OAC)
4511 N. Himes Ave., Suite 250
Tampa, FL 33614
website: www.obesityaction.org

The OAC is a nonprofit organization dedicated to giving a voice to those affected by obesity. It works to eliminate weight bias and discrimination and to improve access to treatment and prevention. Its website contains fact sheets and information about obesity stigma and discrimination.

Obesity Society
1110 Bonifant St., Suite 500
Silver Spring, MD 20910
website: www.obesity.org

The Obesity Society takes a science-based approach to understanding, preventing, and treating obesity. It aims to improve the lives of people affected by obesity. The organization publishes the journal *Obesity*, and its website contains numerous fact sheets about obesity.

State of Obesity
website: http://stateofobesity.org

The State of Obesity is a collaborative project of the Trust for America's Health and the Robert Wood Johnson Foundation, which work to raise awareness about obesity and to encourage prevention. The website contains research papers, fact sheets, maps, and statistics about obesity, as well as the annual *State of Obesity* report.

World Obesity Federation
Charles Darwin 2
107 Gray's Inn Rd.
London WC1 X8TZ
United Kingdom
website: www.worldobesity.org

The World Obesity Federation represents scientific, medical, and research communities around the world and is dedicated to reducing, preventing, and treating obesity. Its website contains fact sheets, tables, and maps about obesity around the world.

For Further Research

Books

Anna Bellisari, *The Anthropology of Obesity in the United States*. New York: Routledge, 2016.

Deborah A. Cohen, *A Big Fat Crisis*. New York: Nation, 2014.

Lee Goldman, *Too Much of a Good Thing: How Four Key Survival Traits Are Now Killing Us*. New York: Little, Brown, 2015.

David A. Kessler, *Your Food Is Fooling You: How Your Brain Is Hijacked by Sugar, Fat, and Salt*. New York: Roaring Brook, 2013.

Robert Paarlberg, *The United States of Excess: Gluttony and the Dark Side of American Exceptionalism*. New York: Oxford University Press, 2015.

Periodicals

Sherzod Abdukadirov and Michael Marlow, "Government Intervention Will Not Solve Our Obesity Problem," *U.S. News & World Report*, June 5, 2012.

Tara Parker-Pope, "The Fat Trap," *New York Times*, December 28, 2011.

Abigail C. Saguy, "If Obesity Is a Disease, Why Are So Many Obese People Healthy?," *Time*, June 24, 2013.

Christopher Snowdon, "Can Public Policy Stop Obesity? The Slippery Slope of Food Regulations," *Cato Unbound*, January 27, 2015.

Internet Sources

Centers for Disease Control and Prevention, "Diabetes 2014 Report Card," 2014. www.cdc.gov/diabetes/pdfs/library/diabetesreportcard2014.pdf.

Nadeem Esmail and Patrick Basham, "Obesity in Canada: Overstated Problems, Misguided Policy Solutions," Fraser Institute, April 2014. www .fraserinstitute.org/sites/default/files/obesity-in-canada.pdf.

Obesity Action Coalition, "Understanding Obesity Stigma," 2015. www .obesityaction.org/wp-content/uploads/Understanding-Obesity-Stigma .pdf.

Allyn L. Taylor and Michael F. Jacobson, "Carbonating the World: The Marketing and Health Impact of Sugar Drinks in Low- and Middle-Income Countries," Center for Science in the Public Interest, February 9, 2016. https://cspinet.org/resource/carbonating-world.

World Health Organization, "Report of the Commission on Ending Childhood Obesity," 2016. www.who.int/end-childhood-obesity/final -report/en.

Index

Note: Boldface page numbers indicate illustrations.

About the Author

Andrea C. Nakaya, a native of New Zealand, holds a BA in English and an MA in communications from San Diego State University. She has written and edited more than forty books on current issues. She currently lives in Encinitas, California, with her husband and their two children, Natalie and Shane.